SUBWAY FIGURE

ALSO BY BRUCE BENNETT

BOOKS
STRAW INTO GOLD
I NEVER DANCED WITH MARY BETH
TAKING OFF *(AN ORCHISES BOOK)*
NAVIGATING THE DISTANCES: POEMS NEW AND SELECTED *(AN ORCHISES BOOK)*
HEY, DIDDLE DIDDLE
FUNNY SIGNALS
THE DESERTED CAMPUS
GRIEF AND LOVE
SOMETHING LIKE KARMA
EPHEMERAE

CHAPBOOKS
COYOTE PAYS A CALL
THE STRANGE ANIMAL
NOT WANTING TO WRITE LIKE EVERYONE ELSE
TO BE A HERON
THE GARDEN & OTHER ABRIDGED VERSIONS
"HER POETRY MANUSCRIPT...IS CURRENTLY CIRCULATING"
BARE BONES
IT'S HARD TO GET THE ANGLE RIGHT
FORAYS
MANEUVERS
GARRETMAN
AH, FIRENZE!
LAST WORDS
SEPARATIONS
BRUCE BENNETT: GREATEST HITS 1962-2000
WERE I TO TELL YOU
MISSING
ETERNAL RECURRENCE AND THE BIG BANG
WEB-WATCHING
MORE LAST WORDS
LATE NIGHT MUSIC
WILL NOBODY STOP THE POET?
COYOTE'S INTERLUDE WITH LITTLE MISS DARLING
EXAMINED LIFE
AGAINST ALL HOPE, I HOPE TO HEAR FROM YOU
VISITATION

SUBWAY FIGURE

•

SUBWAY FIGURE

Talking to no one, no one there to hear,
he rides day after day, year after year,
his goal no destination, no place set,
propelled towards somewhere, nowhere; not there yet.

BRUCE BENNETT

ORCHISES • WASHINGTON • 2009

Library of Congress Cataloging in Publication Data

Bennett, Bruce, 1940-
    Subway figure / Bruce Bennett.
        p. cm.
    ISBN 978-1-932535-21-1
    I. Title.
    PS3552.E54567S83 2009
    811'.54—dc22

                                                    2009011395

ACKNOWLEDGMENTS

Dogwood: "Elusive"; *HUMMINGBIRD:* "Patterns"; *INNISFREE POETRY JOURNAL:* "Against Providence," "False Constructs," "Fictions," "From Surprise To Delight," "Locomotion," "Something Like Karma"; *MEASURE: "Il Bacio*"; *PAINTBRUSH:* "Commitment," "Full Disclosure," "Lowered Expectations"; *RATTAPALLAX:* "The Enemy"; *SMARTISH PACE:* "The Publisher Calls It Quits"; *TAR RIVER POETRY:* "Best Seller"; *THE FORMALIST:* "The Writer's Art"; *The Healing Muse:* "Cycle," "Last Lunch," "Sign Language," "To Someone Who Asked Me After A Poetry Reading How To 'Make It' In Poetry." "Full Disclosure" was published in *Were I To Tell You,* Wells College Press, 2001. "Patterns," "The Examined Life," "Work-In-Progress," "Eternal Recurrence and The Big Bang," were published in the Clandestine Press pamphlet, *Eternal Recurrence and The Big Bang* (2004). "The Publisher Calls It Quits" was published as a Clandestine Press broadside in 2004. The couplets beginning each section were published in *EXAMINED LIFE,* Scienter Press, in 2006.

ORCHISES PRESS
P. O. Box 320533
Alexandria, VA 22320-4533

CONTENTS

COUPLETS *7*

ROMANTIC CHARACTERS

FROM SURPRISE TO
   DELIGHT *9*
ROMANTIC CHARACTERS
   10
THE CORRESPONDENCE
   11
RIDES TOGETHER *11*
REVISIONS *12*
SENSING YOU CHANGE *13*

A SHORT STOP *14*
LATE-NIGHT CALL *14*
VISTA *15*
THOSE TIMES *15*
CONSTANT INCONSTANT
   16
CURIOUS SUITOR *16*
NOW STRANGERS *17*
SOMETHING BETTER *18*

COUPLETS *19*

SOMETHING LIKE KARMA

HOW I STAND *21*
LOCOMOTION *22*
QUARRY *22*
SEEMING *23*
THE ANSWER AND THE
   QUESTIONS *23*
PERFECTION *24*
THE WHEEL *24*
ODD COUPLE *24*
NO CONTROL *25*
AGAINST PROVIDENCE *25*
THE PERSISTENCE
   OF MEMORY *25*
POSSIBILITIES *26*

IDENTITIES *26*
OPEN HOUSE *27*
PRETEND *27*
FICTIONS *28*
DAMAGED GOODS *29*
SMALL EPIPHANY *29*
CONNECT THE DOTS *30*
FALSE CONSTRUCTS *30*
THE MEMORY MACHINE *30*
REMEMBRANCE 31
NO SUCH LUCK 32
THE TERMS *33*
SOMETHING LIKE KARMA
   33

COUPLETS *35*

LOWERED EXPECTATIONS

FULL DISCLOSURE *37*
ON RECEIVING A NOTE
   AND PICTURE FROM
   A FORMER STUDENT
   ANNOUNCING
   SHE HAS BECOME
   A GRANDPARENT *38*
THE PUBLISHER CALLS IT
   QUITS *39*
STILL THE SAME *40*
BELIEVE *41*
SIGN LANGUAGE *43*

ESTATE *43*
BEST SELLER *44*
ELUSIVE *46*
THE ENEMY *46*
THE COMFORT
   OF A MANTRA *47*
JUST LOOKING *48*
IL BACIO 49
LAST LUNCH *50*
LOWERED EXPECTATIONS
   51

COUPLETS *53*

COMMITMENT

TO SOMEONE WHO
   ASKED ME AFTER A
   POETRY READING HOW
   TO "MAKE IT" IN
   POETRY *55*
KEATS'S COMPUTER *56*

SOARING TOWARD
   THE SUN *57*
COMMITMENT *58*
TENNIS, ANYONE?
   59

COUPLETS *61*

CONFLUENCE *63*

ETERNAL RECURRENCE AND THE BIG BANG *64*

CURTAIN CALLS

Sudden reminders flash: a glimpse of hair,
a word you teased me with. And you are there.

*

EMPTY HALL

It's dark. I dance alone. The shadows play.
I offer you my hand. You dance away.

*

PULLING PETALS

"She loves me." *She wants something. It's a plot.*
She's crazy. No, I am. "She loves me not."

*

POSSESSION

To have you yet not have you: now and here
present, yet absent. Torment, far and near!

*

ENDLESS WAR

The battle raged and raged inside my head.
"I am your demon too," my angel said.

ROMANTIC CHARACTERS

FROM SURPRISE TO DELIGHT

You start a poem. You don't know where it's going;
it could go anywhere. It makes a choice.
A course is set. You follow in its flowing,
content to trust its vision and its voice.
Pattern emerges. This will be a sonnet.
It ambles with a clean and easy gait.
You're easy too, though much is riding on it;
you sense significance, a touch of fate.
You start a love affair. Your heart's uncertain.
You don't know where it's leading; nothing's sure.
The stage is set, and life has raised the curtain.
A drama's just beginning. What it's for
is still unclear; the future lies in doubt.
But you sense joy, content to ride it out.

ROMANTIC CHARACTERS

I made it very clear from the beginning:
I was not free; you never could come first.
It was a game you had no chance of winning,
but games are games, and that was not the worst.
We'd have each other in the kind of story
one's thrilled to be a part of. We could play
romantic characters in all their glory,
then stop if there was need to. Oh, the way
we slipped into our roles was cause for wonder!
You were a marvel, blazing and serene;
I was your hero prince. We were not under
the least illusion. It made quite a scene
until, somehow, all lines got mixed or crossed,
and we were what we always were, and lost.

THE CORRESPONDENTS

Set face to face, they stutter and are shy.
Apart, though, and alone, the hot words fly!

*

RIDES TOGETHER

"Let's just keep driving," one of us would say.
Where to? It would not matter. We would be
alone, together, lost and far away:
no plan; no destination; fantasy
transporting us to some new wild location
which would not be a place or have a name.
What did that matter? Only the temptation
was real; the rest was teasing and a game.
We knew we would go nowhere; just a drive,
running some errand, lunch, then heading back.
Yet somehow, as we roared along, alive
in every fiber, feeling that, the lack
of sense or hope was nothing to the high
of watching old, known landscapes rushing by.

REVISIONS

Joking, I called you once "a bitch in heat,"
and you shot back, "Pull over. Let's make love."
That was one dialogue we didn't repeat,
yet one it pleased you to remind me of
later, when you were with someone who said
such things in earnest. With such knowledge then,
I simply would have clasped your hand instead;
I would not play that man not me again.
But did that have to happen as it did?
Were we both doomed to act regretted parts?
Was there no way to change them? Edit bad
lines? Rearrange failed scenes? Avoid misstarts?
Could we have made our drama work, in spite
of all its flaws? Resolve, and get it right?

SENSING YOU CHANGE

Sensing you change, I sought some way to hold you.
It didn't make sense! I didn't know what to do.
I kept it to myself; I never told you,
nor was I even certain that you knew.
Just little things. The ways you seemed distracted;
things were no longer funny: you seemed sad.
Odd chance remarks, and how you sometimes acted
in ways I'd never seen you act. I had
some sense, I guess, that you were growing distant;
that something new was growing in your thought.
But this will pass, I told myself, insistent
that we were strong and solid, that you ought
to work things out yourself. I gave you space
and watched you set another in my place.

A SHORT STOP

We sat and watched the lake.
We didn't have much to say.
It wasn't a mistake.
It simply was the day,

The time, the way the sky
hung lowering and low
like love about to die.
Then it was time to go.

*

LATE-NIGHT CALL

I couldn't make out your words, but you were crying.
I'd never heard such grief. What could I do?
"I've got to give you up." I caught a few.

Transfixed, I felt as if I heard you dying.

I'd play it back. In time, I lost that too.

VISTA

The air is clear
here, without you.

I can see nothing
anywhere

in every direction.

*

THOSE TIMES

Those times when we
stepped out of time,
one being who,
enrapt, sublime,
found out a way
to bliss that few
could know: were they
illusion too?

CONSTANT INCONSTANT

You were so many – are so many now –
real and imagined, it's no wonder how
I cannot place you, shape you, or define
what was, or wasn't, then, or ever, mine.

*

CURIOUS SUITOR

I lived with you intensely in my mind.
You were the thought I woke to; when I slept
I rambled in your company, and kept
gleanings of our adventuring. I'd find
hints of your presence everywhere, and bind
myself to do your bidding; would accept
your least command as law. And if you wept,
I could not be consoled. I was the kind
of curious suitor even I thought odd;
yet I persisted. What was I to do?
In some strange way I turned you into God;
an angel certainly. I prayed to you.
Well, that's all past, and yet I wonder still:
what Power bound me to its force and will?

NOW STRANGERS

I've changed, I know, and you've changed too;
we're not the people who we were.
That man who was in love with you
is gone. That woman? You're not her.

An episode, and we moved on.
That's how it is, and has to be:
a chapter closed; a story done.
We took up different lives; yet we

Would stare in wonder if we met,
and each would marvel at the change,
however prompted to forget,
now strangers, in a world that's strange.

SOMETHING BETTER

To make of something awful something better:
that is how poets earn their keep. Alone
again, I thought: *Suppose I'd never met her?*
My life had been quite placid; it went on
in all the ways it always did. Contented
(as much as anyone) and free from pain,
romance and intrigue (mostly) were invented.
Did I need some real reason to complain?
Or was it something simpler? I was smitten;
a classic case. And she was smitten too.
We played at love, a puppy and a kitten.
Then things turned dark and ugly, as they do.
Both of us suffered. She found what she sought.
I have these poems now. They were dearly bought.

SEMBLANCE

I look around me; all things are a sham.
I look within: *I seem, therefore I am.*

*

THE EXAMINED LIFE?

The answer's simple: simply live. Don't think.
And when the cup of hemlock's offered, drink.

*

PATTERNS

Patterns repeat. We go along.
Hence, crime, Hence, history. Hence, song.

*

PLATFORM

Here. No, here. No, here. Yes, here. Yes, and
yes, also here. And here. Yes, here I stand.

*

THE WAY IT HAPPENED?

The way it happened? Why should that dismay?
I get to tell it. That will be the way.

SOMETHING LIKE KARMA

HOW I STAND

I plant my one foot firmly where
I know I can count on its staying.
My other foot's poised in the air
as if to mount a step, obeying

Another, also stern, injunction:
*Don't let yourself be wholly stuck
in one position, form, or function.*
I count on balance, and on luck.

LOCOMOTION

A snail that makes its sure slow way
persists. It does not need to say:
"My locomotion is okay

For what I do and where I go."
It goes, and does. It isn't "slow."
It has the pace of those who know

Their time's their own, and what they do
is vital, and they'll make it through.
What difference if their tasks are few,

Their track is humble and unseen?
Their fervor for their life is keen!
They have a bead on what they mean.

*

QUARRY

The Answer hovers just beyond my reach.
I know I can't encompass it in speech.
I know That will elude me; still, I set
small traps in words to see what I might get.

SEEMING

What you see is what you get
seems a simple statement; yet
somehow nothing seems to be
quite the thing you seem to see.

*

THE ANSWER AND THE QUESTIONS

The hedgehog knows his world, and knows it well.
It's deep and dark, as far as he can tell.

"Which isn't far at all," his critic mocks.
"You have to know far more to be a fox."

Sometimes these creatures make it up, and switch.
Then neither knows, nor bothers, which is which,

Till both are cast in gloom, and thrown in doubt,
by what they face, and how to work it out.

PERFECTION

The flowers in profusion
beneath a central sun:
perfection. An illusion.
The day is not yet done,

And months lie still before us
of fall, and fall away,
an ever-shrinking chorus
of absence and decay.

*

THE WHEEL

Time is a wheel. Or so they say.
What's past comes round again today
as present, yet it will not last,
except the future is the past.

*

ODD COUPLE

Reason's an errant king. The one who's wise
obliquely riddles in a fool's disguise.

NO CONTROL

The things that happen, happen. No control
is just the order of the day. The whole
resists solicitation. Even prayer
can only second what's already there.

*

AGAINST PROVIDENCE

If accident denotes an act
that did not have to happen, fact
is accidental, only set
by chance that has not happened yet.

*

THE PERSISTENCE OF MEMORY

Why reconstruct what does not last?
Infect the present with the past,
and hold the future hostage too,
consumed by what eluded you?

POSSIBILITIES

If all is meant to be,
and *could* and *can*
are simply destiny,
part of a plan

That none can see or know,
then *might be* too
is part of what is so,
and might be true.

*

IDENTITIES

I am a public person with a name.
The private person is almost the same.
But lurking in the darkness far below
are namelessness and no one that I know.

OPEN HOUSE

I let myself be what I am,
which isn't really me,
although it's also not a sham,
since nothing I can be

Is ever any more than what
each moment brings to bear,
eclipsing all the selves I'm not
whenever they're not there.

*

PRETEND

The actor's not the person he'll become
who's who he'll be when he is acting from
the person who becomes him in the play
that happens only when he goes away.

FICTIONS

The part of anyone you know
is just a part, and even though
your knowledge of that part may grow,

Or, even possibly, extend
to other parts, still, at the end,
it's partial knowledge you depend

Upon to parse into a whole,
a fiction you assign a role,
imagining you can control

That self-created self, which plays
along – or doesn't – knowing ways
to mask the mystery it stays.

DAMAGED GOODS

A self may be illusion,
but that is what you've got.
A mishmash of confusion
it may be, but it's not

Some bad deal you can part with
or trade for one that's new.
The damaged goods you start with
are what must see you through.

*

SMALL EPIPHANY

I read myself for clues to how I act.
I have a small epiphany. In fact,
I see a pattern. Now I simply need
to know how not to act out what I read.

CONNECT THE DOTS

Connect the dots:
the pattern's there,
incipient rev-
elation where

All, all awaits
the mind's quick skill
at gauging what
it means, or will.

*

FALSE CONSTRUCTS

False constructs lead to false conclusions
that lead to greater, worse confusions,
which throw all meaning into doubt
until false constructs sort it out.

*

THE MEMORY MACHINE

No version's perfect, final, or complete.
Reload. Rewind. Hit *Edit,* and repeat.

REMEMBRANCE

The version I come up with next
won't be the final one. I'm vexed
by knowing both what I'm about
and that that won't – and can't – work out,

Since nothing's final, finished, set
in memory. Oh, I'll forget,
believe, be certain that it's sure,
then live the whole charade once more,

Repeating scenes *ad infinit-*
um (while I live), not getting right
what's true, what's not; perplexed because
the past is never what it was.

NO SUCH LUCK

Could we
(of course
we can't)
go back

to what
we were,
I'd bow
and thank

our stars,
then plead
with them
to let

not be
what had
not hap-
pened yet.

THE TERMS

We work with what we have.
We do not choose
the hand we get to play;
yet when we lose,

We cannot claim default
or say the bar
was set by something else
than what we are.

*

SOMETHING LIKE KARMA

Something like Karma makes the only sense.
You live; you die. Yet there is recompense
for how you did it. Something's keeping track.
And, if you're good enough, you don't come back.

33

ILLUMINATION

A flash that may, or may not, be illusion.
The rest is merely chaos and confusion.

*

THE WRITER'S ART

We agonize until we are content
with what we think we thought we might have meant.

*

ACCOMPLISHMENT

I'm what I write; today that comes to this:
a score of words that few will see, or miss.

*

RAID ON THE INARTICULATE

My gamble's this: that in one line, or two,
I'll catch, and hold, what I didn't know I knew.

*

LIFE AS EPIGRAM

Two lines that sum it up. It's done. It's set.
Except for all that has not happened yet.

LOWERED EXPECTATIONS

FULL DISCLOSURE

Were I to tell you what I truly think,
whether in prose or verse, in sign or rhyme,
aloud through words, or silently in ink,
all in a rush, or halting, over time;
Were I to lay all out: my heart, my head,
my deepest mind, my terrors, my conceit;
bundle and send them, to your care consigned;
for your eyes only, naked at your feet;
Were I to do this, and were you to say:
I see; I understand. It's as I dreamed.
There is another being here who may
be just like me. If this were as it seemed,
and we held nothing back, would each possess
new life, or one more lease on loneliness?

ON RECEIVING A NOTE AND PICTURE
FROM A FORMER STUDENT ANNOUNCING
SHE HAS BECOME A GRANDPARENT

Old as the hills, or older yet
I must be, since I now forget
just who this is who shares her joy
about this beaming new-born boy,

This braw and bonnie lad-to-be.
Just what has this to do with me,
except remind me it's a shame
I cannot recollect her name,

Much less her face, or what or when
she learned from me? I learn again,
I barely know from year to year
who leaves, or what they take from here

That makes me part of them enough
to make them want to share the stuff
that happens. Still, it's nice to cherish
the thought that *some* things do not perish.

That what I do, in *someone's* mind,
may leave *some* residue behind;
that someone somewhere's keeping track
of all that is not coming back.

So, thank you for the breaking news.
I'm happy for you, and I choose
not to be sad or glum or grim
that life goes on as I grow dim.

THE PUBLISHER CALLS IT QUITS

"...The truth of the matter, however, is that I'm tired of devoting my
time, energy, and money to the work of others. I'm tired of everyone
wanting to be published but very few wanting to pony up the price of
three or four chapbooks a year...."   *—from a letter*

A thankless task, this editing and printing
of wagonloads of books I cannot sell!
I'll say it loud this time; I'm tired of hinting.
I've had it up to here, if you can't tell.

I'm sick to death of setting type for scrawlers
who write and write. Does anybody *read*?
I've lost my taste for prima donna bawlers.
It's therapy, not publishers, you need.

I'm done. I'm through. I'm taking down my shingle.
I'm outahere. Gone fishin'. Toodle-oo.
You've got a book? Well, you can suck my dingle.
You want some parting words? I've got a few.

In fact, I've got a shitload, in nice covers.
They're cheap as hell and not a one in stores.
Come claim them for yourselves, your Mom, your lovers,
or down the toilet, Bub. And I mean yours.

Your faithful servant's had it. No extension;
no new edition; just one dotted line
that finalizes infinite suspension
of all agreements. One name's on it. Mine.

STILL THE SAME

What can I say? You're dying. I can hear it.
We rarely spoke, and what we said was nil.
You joke about what's coming, but you fear it.
You're still the same, except you're very ill.
I'm still the same: polite and sympathetic,
except I offer nothing; cannot give
my self. Instead, we talk about your medi-
cations, prognosis: Bleak. You will not live,
and we will never delve into estrangement:
how I am you, who took that different way
because of what you taught me, an arrangement
that suited both of us. What can I say?
I'm sorry, yet not sorry. Things occur.
We're still those brothers who we never were.

BELIEVE

Your poems
spread between us

the table
otherwise empty:

"I could die
at any time,"
you say.

*

"I don't believe
in anything":

eyes
unblinking

staring at me

challenging.

*

"I believe
in poetry,"

I say.

"I believe
in what you are doing.

I believe"

I gesture

"in these."

*

The café
remains silent.

You continue
to stare.

There are only
these words
between us.

Only
these words.

SIGN LANGUAGE

You showed me on your wrist
small lines I would have missed,

Thin scars that scored your skin,
but would not let me in

To what was cracked and broken,
to what remained unspoken.

*

ESTATE

It tells us nothing, this proliferation
Of things you did not need but chose to own.
Indulgence? Comfort? Yieldings to temptation?
Buying distractions not to be alone?
We knew all this. We stand amidst the spoils,
Sorting, then cataloguing with a sigh.
Whatever monster held you in its coils,
Whatever whispered, *Now, you have to die,*
That clue's not here. Only this sad accession,
Detritus mixed with articles of worth
We'll sell or give away, as if possession,
Which stands now for your time upon the earth
Were any more than one more missing piece
That galled you toward rejection and release.

BEST SELLER

"I don't *know* if it will be a best seller."
Sharon is talking again about writing a book.
She's found a place that will publish it, for money.
"It's about stuff people will want to read.
Everyday stuff, you know, like about their lives.
The computer can fix my grammar and punctuation."

She's asked before about grammar and punctuation.
I've offered to help. "It might not be a best seller,"
she says again, "but it's about people's lives."
I tell her again, "It's hard to publish a book.
Or rather, it's easy, but not one people will read.
You have to watch out for places that do it for money."

Because, the thing is, she's doing it for the money.
She knows she can get help with punctuation.
She's positive people are going to be eager to read
whatever she writes. "It might not be a best seller,"
but try to tell her it's not going to be a book
that speaks directly to people and changes their lives.

I wish I could help. I know about people's lives,
including Sharon's, and know that she needs the money.
I wish all that could be solved by writing a book,
or even just learning more about punctuation.
It's like some kind of Heaven: you write a best seller;
your life's in lights, and people will pay to read,

And that gives meaning: that people will pay to read.
And, Heaven knows, we need meaning in our lives,
especially the kind that comes as a best seller

written from love and need, not simply for money.
And never mind small details, like punctuation:
one's life's not really one's life till it's in a book!

So Sharon is talking again about writing her book.
"I know it's stuff that people will want to read,
and I can get help with grammar and punctuation."
I guess that's how we all get help with our lives:
we dream what we need to do for love and money.
We feel, *of course* it is in us to write a best seller;

Of course we can publish the book that will change our lives,
that people will want to read, so they'll do it for money.
Who cares about punctuation, when it's a best seller?

ELUSIVE

Hope is the thing with feathers
that flits just out of sight.
I think I might have seen it—
then doubt if I was right.

I think I might have heard it—
then question what I heard.
Each time I come across it,
it is a different bird.

*

THE ENEMY

When young, I knew my enemy was there:
a shape, a figure, in the dark, the air.
Our combat was prescribed, and we knew where.

Of late, I find him harder to discern,
his contours less distinct the more I learn,
his presence sensible at every turn.

THE COMFORT OF A MANTRA

The comfort of a mantra
is how it makes you feel.
Incessant repetition
may not in fact reveal

What caused the consternation
or gives it still its force.
Yet words can summon solace,
as if they were its source.

JUST LOOKING

"… an 18-year-old-redhead in spandex and spike heels…"

-- from a poem

If looking were a crime,
we'd all be doing time.

Decked out, she's *meant* to tempt us,
and nothing can exempt us.

We're men, but not of steel;
our nature is to feel.

We're wired so we treasure
that little surge of pleasure.

There's nothing wrong with knowing,
so long as we keep going.

IL BACIO

an old postcard of Florence

The city's in the background, gray and dim
as if in fog. The lovers, as they kiss,
are all that is in focus: her and him
against the bridge's concrete. Only this,
their image, forms the world for those who view—
pure lust foregrounded, stark against pale light—
the moment deftly caught by someone who,
in passing, saw how passion gripped them, tight,
clinging, each other's all in all, and knew
what they perhaps could not; that moment's bliss,
desperate, oblivious, nothing else in sight,
may be the most that either will possess:
a paradise whose loss they yet must learn.
The fog will lift. The city will return.

LAST LUNCH

for Herbert Siegel

During our last lunch, when you only
pushed food around on your plate, you suddenly
got up because you heard
a couple speaking Greek at the next table

And walked over and introduced yourself and exchanged
pleasantries and information – all
in your best Greek, which was, apparently,
pretty good, or, at least, good enough,

Since you came back beaming. It turned out
he was a doctor, and knew your doctor, and the two of them
complimented you on your knowledge of Greek and asked
where you had acquired it, and you got to tell them

You had always loved languages and had taught
yourself, and it no longer mattered - since you were clearly
so happy – that the food in front of you
would never be eaten, because the restaurant that afternoon

was filled with noise and joy.

LOWERED EXPECTATIONS

When I consider how I've tried and failed –
people, ambitions, projects, dreams – success
always receding; islands never sailed
beyond; expectations becoming less,
until they've faded utterly, replaced
with mundane duties anyone can do;
when facing up, I see what must be faced,
and ruing that, I can't escape that rue,
I tell myself: *Okay then, you were wrong.*
You're not the prodigy you dreamed you'd be.
You're not invincible, or even strong.
You don't add up to much, and what you see
is all there is. Yet, even then, I smile.
I can write this, and this makes that worthwhile.

PUBLIC AND PRIVATE

My life's my life; it is, and is not, fine,
a patchwork compromise. My work is mine.

*

AMAZING

I yield myself to sudden grace. In spite
of knowing nothing, all my steps are right.

*

HIGH WIRE ACT

To balance world on world in phrase on phrase:
such is the mortal game the poet plays.

*

THE WRITING LIFE

To do it and succeed: what joy! But then,
what of it? Gone. It must be done again.

*

ILLUMINATIONS

The glint of wit is not a steady light.
Yet, for an instant, it sets all things right.

COMMITMENT

TO SOMEONE WHO ASKED ME AFTER A POETRY
READING HOW TO "MAKE IT" IN POETRY

I should have told you, "There's no easy way.
You just persist, and do it on your own."
I failed you, though; I didn't know what to say.

You waited, eager-eyed; you clearly stay
hungry for gleanings, desperate to be shown.
I should have told you, "There's no easy way.

You write and write and write, and then one day –
or not – you gather fruit from what you've sown."
Some such old saw. I didn't know what to say,

Because I don't. You struggle, and you pray,
and give it all you've got, and work alone,
and learn quite early there's no easy way

And maybe none at all, but that's okay,
because it's what you choose, and it's the on-
ly thing you want to do. What can one say?

You have this one compulsion. You obey.
You roll your rock. It rolls back down. You groan.
I should have told you, "There's no easy way."
I failed you, though; I didn't know what to say.

The Spell-Check worked, but sometimes he'd forget
to switch it on, and then the "i"s and "e"s
would tumble out reversed, and he would "sieze"
the "momint" – who could fault him, when it let
him hurtle headlong, fiery, on his set
course like a comet! Who'd he have to please
besides himself, and if they chose to tease,
why, he'd laugh too. It had not got him yet.
He still could laugh. The thing was, more and more,
such urgency possessed him: just get down
those words; the letters, lines…. That helped him thrive
in moments when his energy, soon gone,
pummeled him like a kite. He still could soar
in bursts, gulp Heaven's air, and feel alive.

SOARING TOWARD THE SUN

for Caitlin

You're likely to fly off in all directions:
Homer, Kundera, Borges. Who can tell
what principles apply to your selections?
What's most important is, you do it well.
What's less important is, you're hard to follow,
although I try to, skipping far behind.
I like it how you beat the others hollow,
though I can't get a purchase on your mind.
But maybe that is moot. It does not matter
if you're off somewhere, soaring toward the sun,
and I'm left here with literary chatter,
content to view the act when it is done.
We're made so we admire splendid things,
and you are one, aloft, with ah! bright wings.

COMMITMENT

You need to write it till you get it right.
That is your job; what you were born to do.
It might not take a lifetime, but it might.

Sure, it's a burden sometimes, but it's light:
you make the rules, which then apply to you.
That's how you write it till you get it right,

Having that goal, keeping it plain in sight,
yet easing up, or off, since that works too.
It might not take a lifetime, but it might.

At times the task's a breeze, at times it's tight
going, a maze, where every problem's new
and you just need to write to get it right,

Write on, Hell take the cost, by day, by night,
alone, unknown, and yes, the perks are few,
but though it takes a lifetime (and it might),

What's better than commitment to a fight
that brings your best out, focused on what's true?
You have one purpose: Write it till it's right.
It might not take a lifetime. But it might.

TENNIS, ANYONE?

The poet, playing with a net,
has every right to get upset
with those who bend the rules or let

Themselves off easy with the claim
that it is "anybody's game."
He thinks, at least one *ought* to aim

At getting rhyme and meter right!
Yet that's a cause that's lost. Despite
the prime examples he could cite,

Authorities are now too split
on how one ought to write, and wit
is out of favor. Sadly, it

Is clear he cannot hold the fort
alone. He'll have to be a sport
and either share, or leave, the court,

Which, actually, might not be bad,
considering the run he's had.
A champion need not be sad

With all those laurels, knowing too
that if he stays and plays, the new
will, like the old, in time, seem true.

A PHILOSOPHY OF PHILOSOPHIES

The sum of all the ages' earnest chatter?
This life's important, and it does not matter.

*

MERE DREAM

Illusion? All illusion? Can this be
mere dream, as well as what perceives it? Me?

*

BEING ALIVE

This begets that. Things blossom; burgeon; cease.
There's war. Then war. Then war. Then war. Then peace.

*

CYCLE

Love grapples with the darkness. Darkness wins.
There's nothing left to hope for. Hope begins.

*

SPLENDID FINALE

However much the darkness may cast doubt on
"More light! More light!", they're great words to go out on.

CONFLUENCE

I love your poems, Jack Gilbert, but sometimes
they seem mere telling. Not that they don't
make sense. It's just that the sense they make
isn't one anyone can explain, even when the person
has just finished reading the poem. It's like being
in Pittsburgh, where I was one time, looking out
over the water right at the edge of the point
where the rivers come together, roiling in the confluence.
It was dusk. I was alone. I was at a point in my life
where it was going to come together in a new way
but in a way I didn't know then was going to be
different from any way I'd ever thought it would be.
I looked up and saw bats, and I looked around.
The cars on the bridge had already turned on
their headlights, and the first lights on the hills
had started to wink on.

ETERNAL RECURRENCE AND THE BIG BANG

*An accident waiting to happen
again*